Scrap-Appliqué Playground

Turn Quilting Scraps into Fun Appliqué Fabrics

Kay Mackenzie

Martingale®
Create with Confidence

MISSION STATEMENT
Dedicated to providing quality products and service to inspire creativity.

CREDITS
President & CEO: Tom Wierzbicki
Editor in Chief: Mary V. Green
Design Director: Paula Schlosser
Managing Editor: Karen Costello Soltys
Technical Editor: Nancy Mahoney
Copy Editor: Liz McGehee
Production Manager: Regina Girard
Cover & Text Designer: Adrienne Smitke
Illustrator: Robin Strobel
Photographer: Brent Kane

Scrap-Appliqué Playground:
Turn Quilting Scraps into Fun Appliqué Fabrics
© 2012 by Kay Mackenzie

Martingale®
19021 120th Ave. NE, Ste. 102
Bothell, WA 98011-9511 USA
ShopMartingale.com

Printed in China
17 16 15 14 13 12   8 7 6 5 4 3 2 1

Library of Congress Cataloging-in-Publication Data is available upon request.

ISBN: 978-1-60468-139-0

Acknowledgments

A huge thank-you to the staff of Martingale! You're always there with answers for my questions and solutions to my conundrums. Each and every one of you is a pleasure to work with.

Continuing hugs to my husband, Dana Mackenzie, a writer himself, who understands and is with me all the way.

My little dog, Willie, offered his boon companionship every day in the studio during the process of this book, in his self-chosen spot at the base of my stash.

All my quilting friends and fellow appliqué enthusiasts—without you I wouldn't have the best job I ever had, so a great big thank-you for that!

Contents

Greetings

My scrap-appliqué journey started a long time ago, at a rare juncture when I found myself with a little space between deadlines. All I wanted to do was sit down and sew!

I gathered scraps and strips, sorted them into loose colorways, and started sewing them together, cutting across them, and then sewing them together again. It was fun and engaging; I was having a fabulous time with never a thought of what I'd do with those spontaneous fabric compositions. Before I could even get that far, another project came up, so with a little regret I set my free sewing aside, turned my thinker back on, and got back to work on a more focused, planned, thought-out project.

Those patchwork fabric compositions sat in my UFO (unfinished objects) pile for years while I traveled down different roads. But I never discarded them, because I knew that their someday would come. At long last I hauled out those compositions and started playing with the idea of cutting them into appliqué motifs. I made big hearts and stitched some kid quilts for my local charitable group. Those first patchwork hearts were my prototypes, and from them I was able to refine my methods and start on a whole brainstorming session for patched-together appliqué.

Join me on this creative journey. The methods have been refined, but the spontaneous, unplanned aspects remain. These methods are creative and engaging, and you'll have loads of fun putting fabrics together and using your most precious scraps. There's no measuring or calculation, and it's so fulfilling to see the last little bits of some treasured fabric sewn into these projects. So join me on the playground! Turn off your thinker and enjoy the scenery!

Introduction to Scrap Appliqué

What could be more fun than using patched-together pieces for your appliqué? It's the best of both worlds. Patchwork adds a twinkle of visual interest to appliqué motifs. It's engaging, creative, and full of wonderful surprises!

Some of the methods in this book use piecing and some use fusing to create the *Scrap-Appliqué Playground* look. To simplify our terms, we're going to use the word "patchwork" for both pieced and fused compositions.

Not all of the appliqués in a project need to be patchwork. I find that a mix of patchwork and plain motifs works best. And when I say plain, I don't mean drab. The prints you choose for the plain motifs can be as wild and colorful as you like! In this instance, "plain" means regular ol' fabric. Stems, circles, and other small shapes lend themselves well to plain fabrics in these projects.

I started out my quilting life learning to do everything by hand. Over the years I've gradually added machine techniques to my bag of tricks. The work in this book is all done by machine, but of course, feel free to use handwork instead whenever you like.

Many times throughout the instructions you'll be told to press the seam allowances open. Yes, open! This has a two-fold purpose. Most importantly, it will reduce bulk for the appliqués, and pressing the seam allowances open will avoid bowing, which can happen when the seam allowances of strip sets are pressed to one side.

For each project, you'll want to gather your patchwork fabrics. This means pulling the scraps, strips, and fabrics from your stash that you'd like to use for the intended motifs. Let the treasure hunt commence! Choose a variety of bright, dull, light, and dark prints in a variety of scales. A splash of a different color can add a spark. An occasional bias strip is okay; it will be stabilized when sewn to the other strips.

I start with the smallest pieces and work from there. After pulling out small scraps, if I feel I need more, I go through my stash looking for fabrics I can add to the pile. Often, when I pull out a previously cut-into fabric and unfold it, there will be a chunk sticking out that's just begging to be cut off and used. Even if a fabric hasn't been cut into, you have permission. That's what it's there for—to be used!

Gathering the patchwork fabrics is a big part of the fun of this process. I do enjoy a good rummage. It gives me a chance to feel and look at my fabric, which is important to a quilter. You can also use leftover scraps from other projects, scrap bags from the flea market, or scraps begged and traded from your quilting friends. And, I may be the only quilter in the world who's never used them, but you could certainly make use of purchased precut strips, squares, and fat-quarter packs.

How much fabric you'll need is an inexact science; this is a creative, right-brain process and you won't know in advance exactly how many scraps and strips you'll need. Nevertheless, chances are good, gentle quilter, that you have lots of scraps and those that you gather will be plenty enough.

Scrap-Appliqué Methods

We'll use both piecing and fusing methods to create spontaneous fabric compositions for appliqué motifs. I've identified which methods are used for which projects. Once you've got these in your appliqué bag of tricks, feel free to mix and match. Unless otherwise noted, seam allowances are ¼" throughout.

Shrinking Strips

This piecing method uses fabric strips of any length to create hunks of unmatched patchwork. Shorter strips are intentionally sewn to longer strips, making the longer ones shrink as the pairs are cut apart and recombined. The result is a pleasing random composition of squares and rectangles.

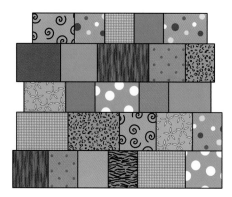

Shrinking Strips is used for the treetops in "Lollipop Park" (page 30) and for the treetops, sun, and ground in "Lollipop Grove" (page 24). For each project using this method, you'll find a pattern for sizing the patchwork compositions as you sew them together. You'll use the pattern and paper or thin cardboard to make a sizing template.

1. Gather and press the patchwork fabrics.

2. Cut the fabrics into strips of varying widths, whatever they will yield. The length of the strips doesn't matter; squares are fine, too. My favorite scale is 2"-, 1¾"-, and 1½"-wide strips, or anywhere in between. You can cut narrower strips if your appliqué motifs are quite small.

When cutting into larger pieces of fabric, it's okay to be conservative at first; you can always go back and cut more strips if you need them. It isn't necessary to trim the ends of the strips perfectly straight; however, do trim off any angled ends.

3. At the sewing machine, pick a long strip. Pick a shorter strip and align it right sides together with the first strip. Sew them together along their long edges. When you reach the end of the top strip, place another strip right sides together with the bottom strip and keep sewing. When you reach the end of the bottom strip, cut off the rest of the top strip and throw it back into the pile of strips. Pick another long strip and repeat.

Don't agonize or plan too much, just keep chain sewing until you've stitched a good number of strips together in pairs. Leave some single strips in case you need fillers later.

4. With scissors, cut the bottom strips apart wherever one top strip ends and another begins. Cut the connecting threads. Press the seam allowances open.

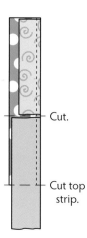

Cut.

Cut top strip.

5. Repeat steps 3 and 4, joining pairs of strips. The strips get shorter and more manageable as you go. Make several strip sets, adding strips until the strip sets are wider than the template (across the width of the strip sets, not the length).

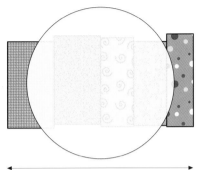

Strip set is wide enough for the project template.

6. Straighten one end of the strip sets and cut into segments, using the same variety of width measurements like in step 2.

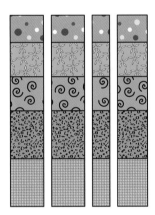

7. Mix up the segments and sew them together, offsetting the seams, until the patchwork composition is larger than your template on all sides. Press the seam allowances open.

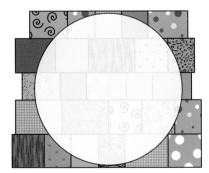

8. Follow the project instructions for making the appliqué elements.

Building Bits and Bobs

"Bits and bobs" is another way of saying bits and pieces or odds and ends. This piecing method starts out the same way as shrinking strips in that it uses fabric strips of any length. However, instead of sewing strips of different lengths together, we'll match up strips of similar length, combine them, rotate them, and then recombine them.

The result is a random piece of patchwork that looks a little bit like an unplanned, free-form Rail Fence unit. A great way to start is with leftover pieces from other projects—remnants of strip sets, piano-key borders, and so on.

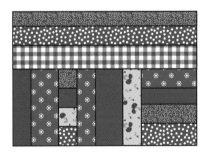

The Building Bits and Bobs technique is used for the letters in "Studio" (page 34) and for the apple and leaves in "Thank You, Teacher" (page 40). For each project using this method, you'll find a pattern for sizing the patchwork compositions as you sew them together. You'll use the pattern and paper or thin cardboard to make a sizing template.

1. Gather and press the patchwork fabrics.

2. Cut the fabrics into strips of varying widths, whatever they will yield. The length doesn't matter; squares are fine, too. My favorite scale is 2"-, 1¾"-, and 1½"-wide strips, or anywhere in between. You can cut narrower strips if your appliqué motifs are quite small.

   When cutting into larger pieces of fabric, it's okay to be conservative at first; you can always go back and cut more strips if you need them. It isn't necessary to trim the ends of the strips perfectly straight; however, do trim off any angled ends.

3. Sort your squares and strips into piles of similar length. For this method the width of the strip doesn't matter.

4. Sew together squares or strips of similar length. Press the seam allowances open.

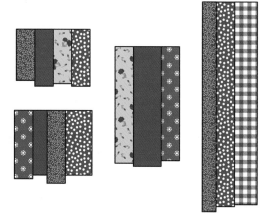

5. When you've sewn a fair number of strips of similar length together or whenever you decide to (remember, we're not planning too much), trim the ends straight across, rotate your patchwork, and sew another strip or another section to the side of your patchwork.

6. Keep sewing and building until the patchwork piece is larger than the project template. It's okay to work quickly and without thinking too much. Don't work so hard at randomizing the fabrics that you lose the enjoyment of the process.

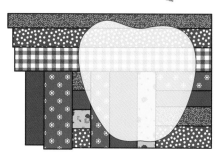

7. Follow the project instructions for making the appliqué elements.

Crazy Patch

This piecing method uses small scraps of fabric of any shape and size sewn together at odd angles, resulting in an unplanned piece of patchwork that looks like an old-fashioned Crazy quilt.

Crazy Patch is used for the beads in "Pop Beads" (page 48) and the hearts in "Crazy Hearts" (page 44). For each project using this method, you'll find a pattern for sizing the patchwork compositions as you sew them together. You'll use the pattern and paper or thin cardboard to make a sizing template.

1. Gather and press the patchwork fabrics. You can use odd-shaped pieces and bias edges for this method.

2. Choose a scrap. Choose another scrap and place it right sides together with the first scrap, at a random angle. Stitch ¼" from the edge of the top scrap.

3. Trim the excess fabric, leaving ¼" for seam allowances. Flip the top fabric over and press the seam allowances open.

4. Place another scrap right sides together with the first two and at a random angle. Stitch.

5. Repeat step 3 to trim, flip, and press the seam allowances open.

6. Continue to build the patchwork piece until it's larger than the project template.

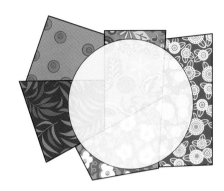

7. Follow the project instructions for making the appliqué elements.

Barber-Pole Bias

This is a very cool and easy way to introduce patchwork into your stems, vines, and, in the case of patchwork-appliqué trees, the trunks! The following instructions are for tree trunks; you can adapt the method for stems and vines in your future projects.

Here's what you'll need before you get started:

- Fabric strips of approximately the same length. Width doesn't matter, but for this application I wouldn't make them any skinnier than 1½".

- Bias press bars made of heat-resistant plastic or aluminum. These come in sets that include a variety of widths. We'll be using the ½"-wide bar for the tree trunks. The plastic bars don't get as hot as the metal ones, making them a little easier to work with.

- Paper-backed fusible tape, ¼" wide. This product can be found alongside the bias-tape makers in the notions section of your favorite quilt shop.

1. Sew the strips together lengthwise. Press the seam allowances open.

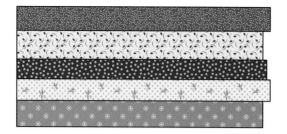

2. To make bias strips that finish ½" wide (as in the tree trunks), crosscut the strip set at a 45° angle, cutting 1½"-wide bias strips.

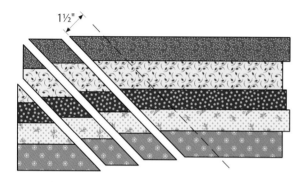

3. You'll end up with pieced bias strips of varying lengths. Cut off the angled ends.

4. Fold the strips in half lengthwise, wrong sides together, and sew with a scant ¼" seam allowance.

Scant ¼"

Fold

5. Insert the press bar, maneuver past the diagonal seam allowances as needed, and rotate the vertical seam so it's centered along the top, flat side of the bar. (If the ½"-wide bar won't fit, use the next smaller size.)

6. Press the seam allowances open, on top of the bar. Gently move the bar along the length of the strip until you've pressed the entire strip.

Bias bar

7. Let the bar cool a bit before touching it so you don't burn your fingers. Then remove the bar and press the fabric tube flat. If the seam allowance extends beyond the sides of the tube, trim it to ⅛".

8. With a hot, dry iron, apply a strip of ¼"-wide fusible tape to the back of each bias strip. Applying the tape now will help the strip hold its shape. Don't remove the paper backing yet.

9. Follow the project instructions for using the strips.

Lay Down and Fuse

This seam-free patchwork method uses small pieces of fabric of any shape and size. It's a great way to use up little pieces of fusible web, too! You'll apply fusible web to the wrong side of your scraps, and then assemble the pre-fused scraps on a nonstick appliqué pressing sheet. Then you'll fuse the assembled scraps together into beautiful, unplanned fabric compositions you can use for your appliqué.

Note: There will be unfinished edges within the appliqué motifs, so reserve this method for decorative projects that won't be washed, and plan on quilting over the motifs.

Here's what you'll need before you get started:

- Fabric scraps (any size and shape is okay)
- Lightweight paper-backed fusible web
- Nonstick appliqué pressing sheet

For each project using this method, you'll find a pattern for sizing the fabric compositions as you lay them out. You'll use the pattern and paper or thin cardboard to make a sizing template.

1. Apply paper-backed fusible web to the wrong side of the fabric scraps using any of the following methods:
   - Roughly match the shapes of your fabric scraps with scraps of fusible web.
   - Cut chunks of fusible web to roughly match the fabric shapes.
   - Use large pieces of fabric and fusible; then cut them into smaller pieces later.
   - Mix and match strategies!

   Just go for it and use what you have in front of you. There are no rules (except that you're not allowed to worry about anything).

2. Once you're ready for the initial fuse, lay the fabric scraps, right side down, on top of a non-stick pressing sheet. Lay the adhesive side of the fusible web on the wrong side of the fabric. With a hot, dry iron, fuse according to the manufacturer's instructions. Leave the paper backing on for now.

3. Let the pieces cool; then cut with scissors just inside the paper edge on all sides. This creates a clean edge and ensures that the fusible is all the way to the edge. Straight or even cutting is not necessary. If the scale calls for it, cut larger pieces into smaller ones. Use the template to roughly judge the size of the pieces as you go.

4. Remove the paper backing from all of the prepared scraps.

5. Lay the scraps, adhesive side down, on top of the pressing sheet, with the edges very slightly overlapped. Create any type of pattern—striped, mosaic, Crazy—improvise, don't agonize. Just have fun and be spontaneous! Keep building until you are satisfied with the arrangement and the composition is larger than the appliqué template.

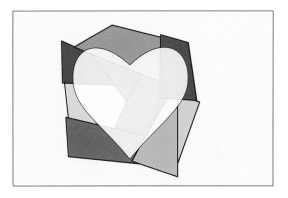

6. Remove the template and press the composition with a dry iron just enough to tack the fabrics together. Don't move the iron back and forth; just pick it up and set it down lightly to tack everything together.

7. Follow the project instructions for making the appliqué elements.

Appliqué-Preparation Methods

Sometimes I think there are about as many ways to appliqué as there are stars in the sky! Let's go over several that are appropriate for our *Scrap-Appliqué Playground* projects.

Turn and Press

This has to be the most direct, no-brainer way to turn an edge and get it ready for stitching! It works great for gentle, flowing curves like the ground and the river in "Lollipop Grove" (page 24) and the grass in "Lollipop Park" (page 30).

The motifs are basted in place on the background fabric. Set your iron on steam. Then simply tuck under the curved edge of the appliqué with your fingers and steam press with the iron. Take care that the steam vents are not directed at your fingers.

Freezer-Paper Templates

Freezer paper, readily available at the grocery store, has long been a staple for appliqué enthusiasts. Freezer paper has a plastic coating on one side that melts slightly with the heat of an iron, allowing it to stick temporarily to fabric.

Traditionally, when using freezer-paper templates, a seam allowance for turning is added when cutting out the appliqué. For the way that we're using the appliqué patterns in this book, a seam allowance is not needed, nor is a reversed pattern.

When directed to make freezer-paper templates, trace the appliqué motifs onto the paper side of the product. To indicate a portion of a piece that is overlapped by another piece, use a dashed line. Roughly cut out the template, not on the drawn line but about ¼" outside the line.

Freezer-paper templates are used for the apple and leaves in "Thank You, Teacher" (page 40) and for the patchwork motifs in "Flower Patch" (page 52) and "Imaginary Blooms" (page 60).

Fusible Interfacing

Fusible-interfacing machine appliqué is a great method for large, simple motifs. Nice smooth shapes are easy to achieve, the edges are turned, and the motifs are held securely in place for edgestitching or the machine stitch of your choice. Then the interfacing is trimmed away, leaving no bulk or stiffness.

The fusible-interfacing method is used for the treetops, sun, and birds in "Lollipop Grove" and "Lollipop Park" and the beads in "Pop Beads" (page 48). It's also suitable for the hearts in "Crazy Hearts" (page 44) if you choose. For this method, you'll want to be sure you're using fusible *interfacing* (which has adhesive on one side only), not fusible web (which fuses on both sides). Fusible interfacing comes from the garment-sewing world. It has a smooth side and a slightly bumpy side. The marking is done on the smooth, nonfusing side. A reversed pattern is not needed. When first using the product, take a moment to familiarize yourself with the feel of the two sides.

Here's what you'll need before you get started:

- Sheer to lightweight nonwoven fusible interfacing
- Thin, stiff cardboard to make a tracing template
- Straight pins
- Pointy implement for turning, such as a chopstick, knitting needle, or the end of a spoon (if your spoons have handles with pointy ends)

In the following instructions, I'll show you how to make a circle.

1. Use the circle pattern on page 50 and thin cardboard to make a circle template.

2. Using a pencil or fabric marking pen, trace the circle onto the *smooth side* of a square of interfacing.

3. Place the marked interfacing square, *smooth side up,* on the *right side* of a square of scrap fabric. Pin the layers together in a few places. (After practicing, you may find you don't need the pins.)

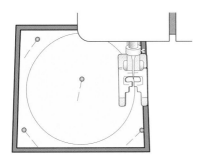

4. Slowly sew around the circle, using a short stitch length and stitching just inside the marked line. Pivoting should not be necessary. Stop with the needle in the down position when you need to pause and reposition your hands. Sew a few stitches past where you started.

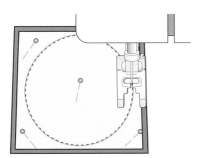

SMOOTH CIRCLE SEWING TIP

Try placing your left hand flat on the unit and rotating it counterclockwise as you sew. If you have trouble, try sewing slower or shortening the stitch length.

5. Trim the seam allowances to about ⅛". Pull the interfacing away from the fabric. Pinch a fold in the center of the interfacing and make a nip through the fold with the tip of your scissors. Then lengthen the slit just enough to turn the circle right side out through the opening.

6. Once the circle is turned, insert the pointy implement through the opening and run it along the stitching line, fully extending the seam and smoothing out the curve. The circle will be a little puffy, but *do not* press with an iron until you're ready to fuse.

7. Using white thread, hand sew a few basting stitches through the interfacing to pull the slit together and prevent the interfacing from peeking out around the edge of the appliqué fabric.

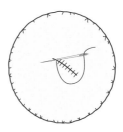

8. When you're ready to fuse the motif in place, place the circle, fabric side up, on the right side of the background fabric (or square). Using a hot iron with steam, fuse the circle in place, following the manufacturer's instructions for the interfacing. Don't move the iron back and forth; hold it in place, lifting the iron and repositioning

it until the entire circle is flattened and fused. Let cool.

9. Edgestitch or use the machine stitch of your choice to secure the edges of the fused circle.

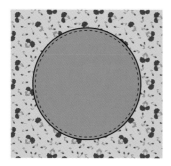

10. Since the interfacing is fused only to the background fabric and not to the circle, you can remove the layers of fabric and interfacing underneath the circle to reduce bulk. Pull the fused background away from the circle. Pinch a fold in the background and make a nip through the fold. Use scissors to carefully trim away the fused background layer, leaving a scant ¼"-wide seam allowance or enough to cover the turned edge of the circle.

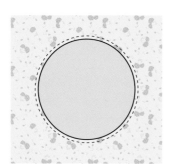

Fusible-Web Templates

Raw-edge fusible-web appliqué is a widely used method among appliqué enthusiasts. I use it for both patchwork and plain motifs, depending on the project. With this method, your finished appliqué will be a mirror image of the pattern that you use for making templates. In this book, all asymmetrical patterns for fusible-web shapes are shown in reverse for your convenience, except the patterns for "Flower Patch" on page 52. Symmetrical patterns do not need to be reversed.

Here's what you'll need before you get started:

- Lightweight paper-backed fusible web
- Scissors that you don't mind using to cut paper

1. Each motif needs its own template. Trace each appliqué motif individually onto the paper side of the fusible web, leaving at least ½" between motifs. A pencil is fine for this. To indicate a portion of a piece that is overlapped by another piece, use a dashed line.

2. Roughly cut out each template about ¼" outside the lines.

3. To reduce stiffness in the finished quilt, remove the center portion of all but the smallest templates. Cut through the edge of each template to about ¼" inside the drawn line and trim away the center, leaving a ring of fusible web in the shape of the motif.

4. Using a dry iron and following the manufacturer's recommendations, press the templates *fusible side down* onto the *wrong* side of the patchwork or plain fabric.

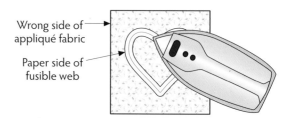

Wrong side of appliqué fabric

Paper side of fusible web

5. Allow the fabric and templates to cool briefly. Cut out the motifs exactly on the solid pencil lines. Leave a little fabric outside any *dashed* lines.

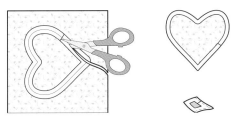

6. Follow the project instructions for using the appliqué elements.

Bias-Covered Edges

This method is closely akin to the appliqué style called stained glass, except that you can choose to make the bias tape in the same color family as the motif. You'll need:

- ¼" bias-tape maker
- ¼" paper-backed fusible tape
- Glass-head straight pins

To make bias tape, I reach for my trusty gadget—the ¼" bias-tape maker. This tool automatically folds the edges of the fabric to make bias tape that is a nice even width.

Here's how I get the bias-tape maker to work easily for me:

1. For the ¼"-wide gadget, cut a ⅝"-wide strip of fabric on the bias. Trim the top of the strip at an angle upward to the left. (It seems to feed through the gadget better this way.)

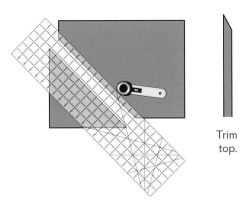

Trim top.

If you don't need a flexible strip that can curve and meander, you can simply cut the strips on the straight of grain instead of on the bias (they wiggle less) and cut one end at an angle.

2. Poke the pointed end of the strip, right side up, into the gadget until you can see the fabric in the slot on top. Use the tip of a pin to pull the strip along the slot until it sticks out the narrow end of the tape maker. Pin this folded end of the strip to the ironing board. Don't use a plastic-headed pin; it can melt from the heat of your iron.

3. Using a hot iron and plenty of steam, pull the gadget along the strip with one smooth, fairly rapid motion, following it closely with the iron. *Hold your iron so that the steam vents are not directed at your fingers.* Don't stop partway through or try to back up. Pulling smoothly is important for getting nicely formed bias tape.

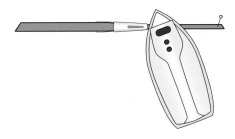

4. Make the bias strips fusible by applying a strip of paper-backed fusible tape to the back of each strip. The product comes on a roll and can be found alongside the bias-tape makers in the notions section of your favorite quilt shop. I apply the fusible tape with a dry iron as a separate step, right after making the bias tape.

5. When ready to apply the bias tape to the project, remove the paper backing and fuse the tape in place with a hot steam iron, molding the tape along curves.

BIAS-TAPE MAKER WON'T WORK FOR BARBER-POLE BIAS

I tried making Barber-Pole Bias strips, as shown on page 11, with my trusty gadget, but the seam allowances made the strips too bulky to go through the device. That's why I pulled out the bias press bars for them.

Stitching Methods

For machine appliqué, I use edgestitching for turned-edge shapes and a machine blanket stitch for raw-edge shapes. You can certainly use other stitches, such as zigzag or even a hand blanket stitch, to finish the edges of your appliqués if you like.

Edge Stitch

For super-simple edge stitching, use thread that matches or blends with the fabric. Shorten your stitch length and sew on top of the appliqué shape as close to the edge as possible. Pivoting should not be necessary. Stop with the needle down when you need to pause and reposition your hands. If you have trouble, try sewing slower or use a shorter stitch length.

When you return to where you started stitching, sew over a few stitches and then backstitch to secure the threads.

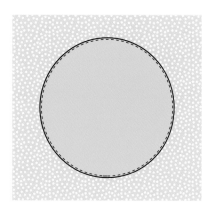

Blanket Stitch

Many machines have a built-in blanket stitch. If yours doesn't, you can use a zigzag stitch instead.

Here's what you'll need before you get started:

- Sewing machine with either a blanket stitch or an adjustable zigzag stitch
- Open-toed presser foot
- Sharp machine needle in a small size, such as 70/10
- Thread: I use a fine thread, usually 50-weight, two-ply cotton thread in a matching color. Use a contrasting color or a heavier thread if you prefer a more defined look for the edges of your appliqués.

Start by testing your stitching on a scrap project. Experiment with stitch length and width until you're satisfied with the tension and the appearance of the stitching.

For blanket stitching, the length of the forward stitch and the sideways stitch should be the same. The forward stitches go into the background fabric, right next to the motif. The sideways stitches bite into the motif at a right angle to the edge.

Start stitching where a motif just emerges from underneath another one, and end where it goes back under. Sew slowly and steer around curves as much as you can. When you need to pivot, stop with the needle down in the background fabric. Raise the presser foot, pivot the project, lower the presser foot, and continue sewing. Around tight curves, it's better to make frequent small pivots than fewer large ones. Use strategic pivoting to keep the sideways stitches biting into the motif at a right angle, including points and notches.

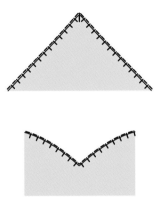

I'm fond of matching the thread to the motif. If you do this too, sew all areas of one color—such as all the pink—before changing threads and moving on to the next color.

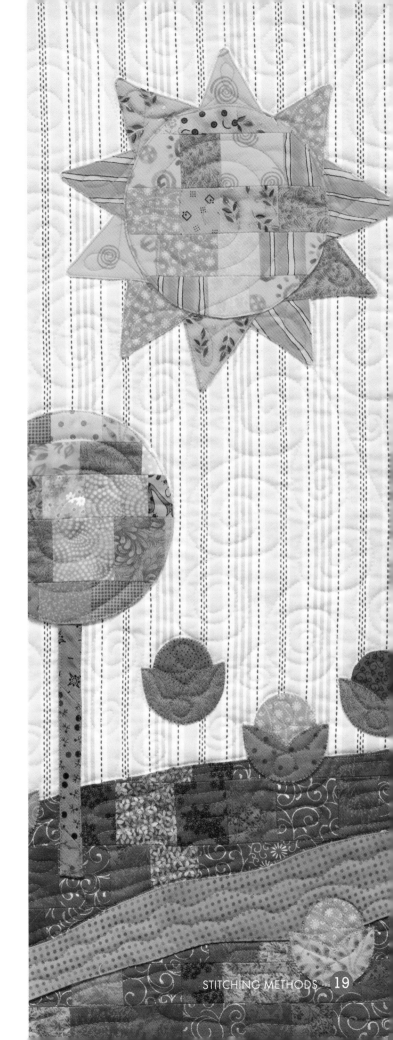

The Finish Line

You've sewn that last stitch on your quilt top. What a sense of accomplishment. It's done! Yes! No! Not really. There are still the finishing steps. Here's how I turn a quilt top into a finished quilt.

Layering and Basting

The backing fabric and batting should extend 1" or 2" beyond the quilt top all the way around. I use low-loft cotton batting, but you may use the batting of your choice. Press the backing fabric and lay it out flat, wrong side up. Use tape or pins to secure the backing in place on the floor or a table. Layer the batting on top of the backing and smooth out any wrinkles. Center the quilt top over the batting and backing. Use size 0 brass safety pins to pin baste all the layers together, placing the pins about every 4" in a grid.

Confession time: On small projects, I've been known to baste with straight pins. It's quicker, but it's also a good way to stab yourself.

Quilting

As noted previously, I started out my quilting life doing everything by hand. It was quite a process for me to learn machine quilting. Practice, practice, practice, and then practice some more! I still make no great claims as a machine quilter, but I've gotten to the point where I've developed my own quirky quilting ways and can do a respectable job.

I free-motion outline quilt around my appliqués, and I use a walking foot for in-the-ditch quilting. I'm not afraid of changing thread colors and I enjoy quilting on top of my appliqués, particularly when I use my Lay Down and Fuse method (page 12). It's important to quilt over these appliqués, because there are raw edges within the motifs, and the quilting will help secure them.

For background-fill quilting, I use a lot of spirals, which is a start-and-stop pattern. I enjoy it, but I wouldn't inflict it on anyone else! Use the quilting patterns of your choice to finish your quilts.

Binding

I use bias binding. I'm convinced that the slight amount of elasticity in the bias helps pull in any tendency a border may have to wave. You can certainly use straight-of-grain binding if you prefer. I've used it a time or two myself, in a pinch.

For the small projects in this book, I cut 2"-wide bias strips and used a 1/4" seam allowance. You can cut your strips slightly wider and use a wider seam allowance if you prefer. Just make sure that when the binding is folded to the back of the quilt, the folded edge covers the line of machine stitches.

MAKING THE BINDING

1. From the pressed fabric, cut 2"-wide bias strips.

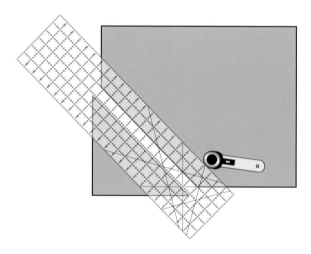

2. Trim the ends of the bias strips straight across at a 90° (right) angle.

3. Overlap the strips, right sides together, at a 90° angle with the raw edges aligned. Sew diagonally across the strips as shown.

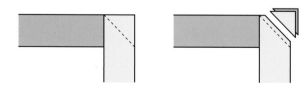

4. Continue joining strips in the same manner until the strip is long enough to go all around the quilt, plus 8" to 10" for mitering the corners and joining the strips at the end. Trim the excess fabric, leaving a scant ¼" seam allowance.

5. Press the seam allowances open. Fold the binding in half lengthwise, wrong sides together, and press.

APPLYING THE BINDING

You may already have your binding technique down pat. I've developed my own way of joining the ends that involves trimming away bulk and stitching by hand. Here's how I apply binding if you'd like to give it a whirl:

1. With the fold of the binding to the left and the raw edges to the right, trim a triangle-shaped section from the beginning end of the binding as shown. Be sure to cut the top layer only, leaving the bottom layer intact.

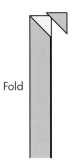

Fold

2. Fold the left corner down at a 45° angle and press. Trim the folded section, leaving a scant ¼" seam allowance.

3. Starting in the middle on one side, align the raw edges of the binding with the raw edges of the quilt front. Using a ¼" seam allowance, stitch the binding to the quilt; stop sewing ¼" from the corner with a backstitch. Remove the quilt from the machine and clip the threads.

4. Turn the quilt so that you'll be stitching along the next side. Fold the binding up, away from the quilt, creating a 45° angle at the fold. Holding the fold in place, bring the binding back down onto itself; align the edge of the binding with the next edge of the quilt. Starting at the fold with a backstitch, continue sewing the binding to the quilt, mitering each corner as before.

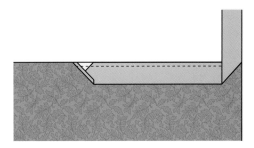

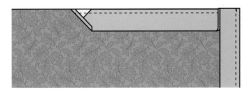

5. When you near the starting point, place a pin where you started stitching.

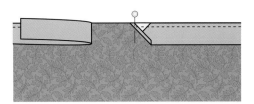

6. Overlap the binding tails and sew two or three stitches past the pin, then backstitch.

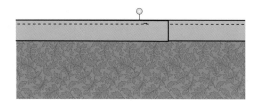

7. Remove the pin and remove the quilt from the sewing machine.

8. Fold the binding away from the quilt. Where the binding overlaps, hand sew along the fold using matching thread and a small blind stitch.

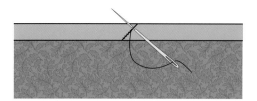

9. Trim the excess binding, leaving a ¼" seam allowance where the binding overlaps. Fold the binding over the raw edges of the quilt to the back, with the folded edge covering the row of machine stitches. Hand stitch in place, mitering the corners.

Making a Framed Label

When I'm making a quilt, I keep the leftover fabrics handy until I'm totally done with the project. It's fun to use leftovers from the front of the quilt to frame the label on the back.

You can include lots of information on your label, such as the personal story of how your quilt came to be made. At the very least, include the quilt's name, your name, and the date, as I've done here. If you're putting your quilt in a show, the show rules may have labeling requirements, such as including address and phone number.

I use a permanent fabric marker to write the information on the label. Then I back the label with another piece of light fabric to prevent the backing fabric from showing through. I sew strips of fabric onto the label to make a simple frame, sides first, and then top and bottom (or the other way around). You can use the same fabric on all four sides, one fabric for the sides and a different fabric for the top and bottom, or four different fabrics.

Press under ¼" all the way around the edges of the label, baste it to the back of the quilt, and hand stitch in place, sewing through the backing fabric only.

Lollipop Grove

Lollipop trees grow from rich, patched earth in a quiet river grove. The ground reminds me of growing up in Orange County. No, not the famous Orange County in California, but the one in North Carolina, where red clay is found everywhere. Wherever you live, this project offers a great combo platter of scrap-appliqué and stitching methods to make this happy little stand of lollipop trees.

Finished Quilt: 35½" x 25½"

PLAYGROUND METHODS USED

* Shrinking Strips (page 8) for treetops, sun circle, and ground
* Barber-Pole Bias (page 11) for tree trunks
* Fusible Interfacing (page 14) for treetops, sun circle, sun rays, and birds
* Fusible-Web Templates (page 16) for gumball flowers
* Turn and Press (page 14) for ground and river

Materials

⅞ yard of striped fabric for background

5" x 40" strip **OR** ¼ yard of blue fabric for river

Scraps of 4 assorted light-brown fabrics, at least 4" x 13", for tree trunks

Scraps of 4 assorted dark-brown fabrics, at least 4" x 13", for tree trunks

Scraps of assorted green, brown, blue, red, orange, yellow, gold, and brown fabrics for patchwork and plain appliqués

⅜ yard of fabric for binding

⅞ yard of fabric for backing

29" x 39" piece of batting

¾ yard of 20"-wide sheer to lightweight fusible interfacing for trees and sun

¼ yard of 17"-wide lightweight paper-backed fusible web for gumball flowers

¼"-wide paper-backed fusible tape for tree trunks

Bias press bars for tree trunks

Black permanent fabric marker for bird beaks*

Thin cardboard for circle template

Chalk marker

6 to 7 pieces of plain paper

*Be sure to use a pen that doesn't bleed, such as a Pigma pen or Marvy marker.

Cutting

From the striped fabric, cut:
1 rectangle, 27" x 37"*

From *each* of the assorted light-brown scraps, cut:
1 strip, 3" x 12" (4 total)

From *each* of the assorted dark-brown scraps, cut:
1 strip, 3" x 12" (4 total)

From the binding fabric, cut:
130" of 2"-wide bias strips

If the fabric is directional like the background in my project, make sure the cutting orientation is correct.

Making the Appliqué Elements

You'll start by making all of the patchwork and plain appliqué elements.

TREETOPS

1. Using thin cardboard and the tree-and-sun pattern on page 29, make a circle template.

2. Make 10 green patchwork compositions using the Shrinking Strips method. Make some lighter treetops and some darker treetops. Use the template to make sure each composition is larger than the circle.

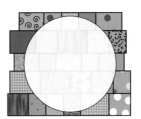

3. Use the Fusible Interfacing method and the circle template to make 10 lollipop treetops. Do not press the treetops until you are ready to fuse them to the background.

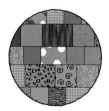

TRUNKS

1. Sew the four light-brown strips together to make a strip set. Press the seam allowances open. Sew the four dark-brown strips together to make a second strip set; press.

2. Use the Barber-Pole Bias method to make seven light-brown tree trunks and three dark-brown tree trunks. (Feel free to make any combination of light and dark tree trunks.)

SUN

1. Using the Shrinking Strips method, make an orange and yellow fabric composition for the sun center using the same template as for the treetops.

2. Use the Fusible Interfacing method and the patchwork composition to make one sun center.

3. Use the Fusible Interfacing method and the sun-ray pattern on page 29 to make 10 sun rays from the orange and yellow scraps. Leave the curved edge of the sun rays open for turning. Trim the seam allowances, being sure to leave about ¼" beyond the dashed line. At the point, taper the seam allowances to ⅛" at the tip. Instead of cutting a slit in the interfacing, simply turn the rays through the open section. Use a pointy implement to gently poke out the tips, being careful not to poke all the way through.

NIFTY POINT

Here's a tip I learned in eighth-grade home-ec class. At the tip of each sun ray, stop with the needle in the down position, pivot halfway, sew one stitch across the tip, then pivot again, and keep sewing. This gives a little extra room in the tip for the seam allowance once the shape is turned.

BIRDS

The birds are made from plain fabric. Using the patterns on page 29 and the Fusible Interfacing method, make one red bird and one blue bird.

GROUND

1. Make a full-sized paper template for the ground, taping pieces of paper together as needed. The curve and slope of the ground doesn't need to be exactly like mine, so the upper outline of the template can be very approximate.

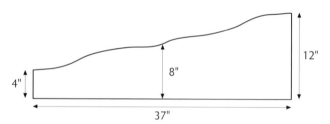

2. Using the Shrinking Strips method, use the red, orange, gold, and brown fabrics to make a patchwork composition for the ground. Build the composition until it's large enough to fit the dimensions of the paper template.

GUMBALL FLOWERS

The flowers and leaf bases are made from plain fabrics. Use the Fusible-Web Templates method and the patterns on page 29 to make nine flowers and nine leaf bases from assorted scraps.

Putting It All Together

1. Lay the background rectangle, right side up, on the ironing board. Lay the ground composition, right side up, on top of the background, aligning the bottom edges.

2. Draw a gently curving, sloped chalk line denoting the top edge of the ground. You can use your paper template or free-hand draw the edge if you like.

3. When satisfied with the edge, hand baste the ground to the background fabric, about 1" below the chalk line. With scissors, trim the top edge of the ground about ¼" above the chalk line.

4. Lay the blue river strip across the ground. Use the chalk marker to draw the river's top and bottom edges in gentle, flowing curves.

5. When satisfied with the river, hand baste about 1" inside each chalk line. With scissors, trim the river fabric, leaving about ¼" outside each chalk line.

6. Use the Turn and Press method to prepare the edges of the ground and river for stitching. Edgestitch along the turned edges. Remove the basting.

7. Turn the project over and trim away the background fabric from underneath the ground, leaving about ¼" for seam allowance.

8. Refer to the photo on page 25 as needed for placement guidance. Arrange the treetops, tree trunks, birds, sun, and gumball flowers on the background as desired. Following the manufacturers' instructions, fuse all elements in place on the background, turning under the bottom edges of the tree trunks before fusing.

9. Edgestitch the trees, sun, and birds. Blanket-stitch the flowers. To reduce bulk, cut away the fused background underneath each fusible-interfacing element.

10. Draw the bird beaks with a permanent fabric marker.

11. Trim and square up the edges of the quilt top. Your "Lollipop Grove" may end up a somewhat different size than mine. That's perfectly okay—it's your grove!

12. Stay stitch ⅛" inside the outer edge of the ground section. This will keep the seams intact during the quilting and finishing process.

The Finish Line

Refer to "The Finish Line" on page 20 for information on how I finish my quilts. Layer, baste, quilt, and bind your project. Add a label.

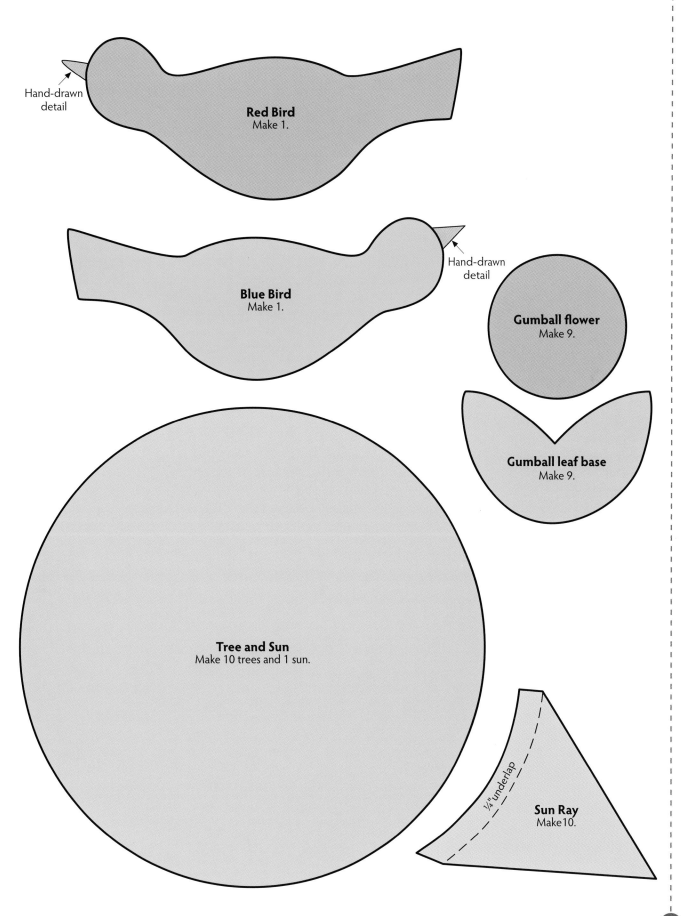

Hand-drawn detail

Red Bird
Make 1.

Blue Bird
Make 1.

Hand-drawn detail

Gumball flower
Make 9.

Gumball leaf base
Make 9.

Tree and Sun
Make 10 trees and 1 sun.

¼" underlap

Sun Ray
Make 10.

Lollipop Park

Under the seting sun, plump birds fly home to their patchwork trees in the lollipop park.

Finished Quilt: 28½" x 11½"

PLAYGROUND METHODS USED

* Shrinking Strips (page 8) for treetops
* Barber-Pole Bias (page 11) for tree trunks
* Fusible Interfacing (page 14) for treetops, sun circle, sun rays, and birds
* Turn and Press (page 14) for grass

Materials

½ yard of blue fabric for sky

¼ yard of green fabric for grass

Scraps of 4 assorted brown fabrics, at least 4" x 13", for tree trunks

Scraps of assorted green fabrics for patchwork treetops

Scraps of assorted orange and yellow fabrics for sun

Scraps of assorted red fabrics, at least 3" x 5", for birds

⅜ yard of fabric for binding

½ yard of fabric for backing

15" x 32" piece of batting

¼ yard of 20"-wide sheer to lightweight fusible interfacing for treetops, birds, and sun

¼"-wide fusible tape for tree trunks

Black permanent fabric marker for bird beaks*

Thin cardboard for circle template

Chalk marker

*Be sure to use a pen that doesn't bleed, such as a Pigma pen or Marvy marker.

Cutting

From the blue fabric, cut:
1 rectangle, 13" x 30"

From *each* of the assorted brown scraps, cut:
1 strip, 3" x 12" (4 total)

From the ¼ yard of green fabric, cut:
1 strip, 4" x 30"

From the binding fabric, cut:
88" of 2"-wide bias strips

Making the Appliqué Elements

You'll start by making all of the patchwork and plain appliqué elements.

TREETOPS

Refer to the treetop diagrams on pages 25 and 26 as needed.

1. Using thin cardboard and the tree pattern on page 33, make a circle template.

2. Use the Shrinking Strips method to make three green patchwork compositions. Use the template to make sure each composition is larger than the circle.

3. Use the circle template and the Fusible Interfacing method to make three lollipop treetops. Do not press the treetops until you're ready to fuse them to the background.

TRUNKS

1. Sew the four brown strips together to make a strip set. Press the seam allowances open.

2. Use the Barber-Pole Bias method to make three tree trunks.

SUN

1. Use the Fusible Interfacing method and the patterns on page 33 to make one quarter-circle sun and three sun rays from the orange and yellow scraps. Leave the dashed-line portions open for turning. Refer to "Nifty Point" on page 26 for a tip on stitching the sun-ray points. Trim the seam allowances, being sure to leave about 1/4" beyond the dashed line. At the point of each sun ray, taper the seam allowances to 1/8" at the tip.

2. Turn the elements through the open sections. On the sun rays, use a pointy implement to gently poke out the tips, being careful not to poke through the tip.

BIRDS

The sitting bird pattern is on page 29 and the flying-bird pattern is on page 33.

The birds are made from plain red scraps. Use the Fusible Interfacing method to make one sitting bird and three flying birds.

Putting It All Together

1. Lay the blue rectangle, right side up, on the ironing board. Lay the green grass strip, right side up, on top of the sky, aligning the bottom edges.

2. Use a chalk marker to draw the finished dimensions of the quilt, 28" x 11", on the grass and sky. On the green strip, draw a gently curving chalk line denoting the top edge of the grass. The curve and slope of the grass don't need to look exactly like mine. At its highest point, my grass is 2½" tall; at its lowest, ¾" from the bottom finished edge.

3. When satisfied with the grass line, hand baste the grass to the sky background, about 1" below the chalk line. With scissors, trim the top edge of the grass about ¼" above the chalk line.

4. Use the Turn and Press method to prepare the top edge of the grass.

5. In the upper-left corner, position the sun, making sure the seam allowance extends beyond the finished-size markings. Remove the paper backing from the tree trunks and position all elements as desired, tucking the ends of the tree trunks under the edge of the grass. Refer to the photo on page 31 as needed for placement guidance.

6. Following the manufacturer's instructions, fuse all elements in place. Edgestitch all of the elements.

7. To reduce bulk, cut away the fused background from underneath each fusible-interfacing element.

8. Draw the bird beaks with a permanent fabric marker.

The Finish Line

Refer to "The Finish Line" on page 20 for information on how I finish my quilts. Layer and baste the project. Quilt the project, keeping the quilting inside the finished-size markings. Trim the project, leaving a ¼" seam allowance beyond the finished-size marking on all sides. Add binding and a label.

Your "Lollipop Park" may be a slightly different size than mine. That's perfectly okay—it's your park!

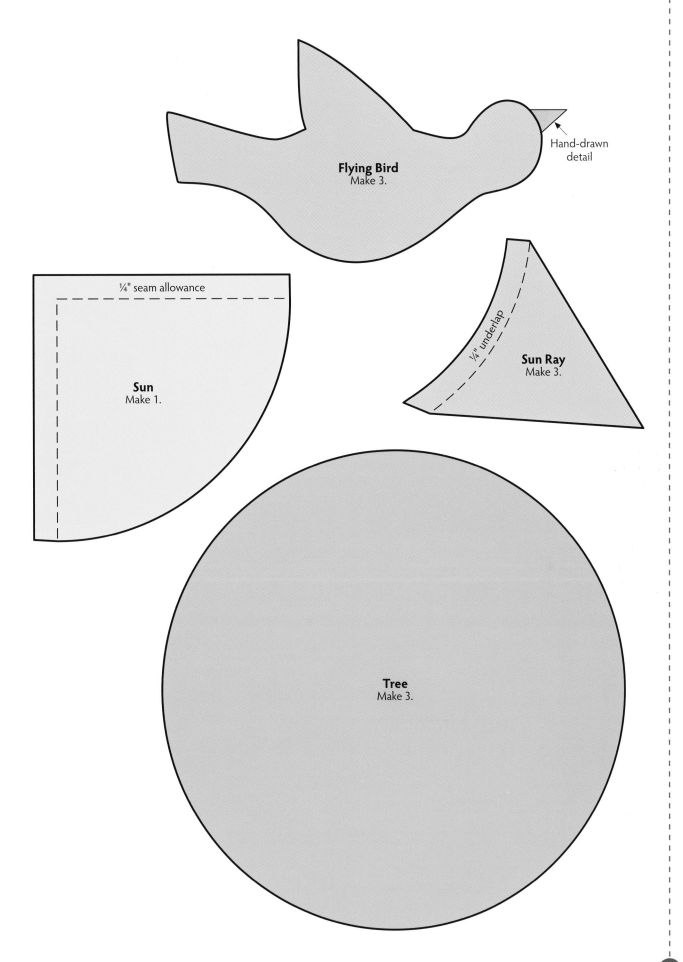

Flying Bird
Make 3.

Hand-drawn detail

¼" seam allowance

Sun
Make 1.

¼" underlap

Sun Ray
Make 3.

Tree
Make 3.

Studio

I made this quilted sign to hang in my sewing room, thereby elevating its status to a "studio." If you make a sign for your sewing room, it can be a studio, too!

Finished Quilt: 30½" x 12½"

PLAYGROUND METHODS USED

* Building Bits and Bobs (page 9) for letters
* Fusible-Web Templates (page 16) for letters, spool, and scissors

Materials

½ yard of white print for background

Scraps of assorted black, white, and red prints for patchwork letters and border

Scraps of red fabric for spools of thread and scissor handles

Scrap of gray fabric for scissor blades

Scrap of red dot print for flower

Scraps of black solid for spool ends

⅜ yard of fabric for binding

½ yard of fabric for backing

16" x 34" piece of batting

½ yard of 17"-wide lightweight paper-backed fusible web

1 gray button, ⅜" diameter, for scissor hinge

3 pieces of plain paper

Cutting

From the white print, cut:
1 rectangle, 27" x 11"

From the assorted black, white, and red prints, cut a *total* of:
50 rectangles, 1½" x 2½"

From the binding fabric, cut:
95" of 2"-wide bias strips

Making the Appliqué Elements

1. Trace the letters on pages 36–38 onto plain paper and cut them out to use as sizing templates.

2. Use the Building Bits and Bobs method and the assorted black, white, and red scraps to make six fabric compositions. Use the paper templates to make sure each composition is larger than the letter.

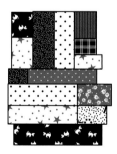

3. Using the Fusible-Web Templates method, the letter patterns on pages 36–38, and the patchwork compositions, prepare the letters. Use the patterns and assorted scraps to prepare three spools, one flower, one flower center, and one pair of scissors.

Making the Quilt Center

1. Arrange the letters and other elements as desired on the background fabric. Refer to the photo above for placement guidance. Notice that I slightly offset every other letter in an up-and-down fashion, just for fun. Be sure to position the elements at least ½" from the outer edges of the background fabric on all sides to allow for seam allowance and trimming.

2. Fuse the elements in place, and then blanket-stitch around each one. I used black thread on the letters and matching thread on the spools, flower, and scissors.

3. Press the quilt top. Trim the quilt top to measure 26½" x 10½", keeping the design centered.

Making the Border

1. Lay out the 1½" x 2½" black, white, and red rectangles as shown at right to frame the quilt center.

2. Sew 13 rectangles together end to end to make the top border. Repeat for the bottom border. Press the seam allowances open. The borders should measure 26½" long. If they don't, adjust a few seam allowances to achieve the desired length.

3. Join the top and bottom borders to the quilt. Press the seam allowances toward the border.

4. Sew 12 rectangles side by side for each side border. Press the last seam allowances on each side toward the center of the borders. Press the remaining seam allowances open. The borders should measure 12½" long. If they don't, adjust the seam allowances as needed.

5. Sew the side borders to the quilt top, matching seam intersections. Press the seam allowances toward the border.

6. Stay stitch ⅛" inside the outer edge of the border. This will keep the seams intact during the quilting and finishing process.

The Finish Line

Refer to "The Finish Line" on page 20 for information on how I finish my quilts. Layer, baste, and quilt the project. Add binding and a label. Sew the button on the scissors for the hinge.

Patterns are reversed
for fusible appliqué.

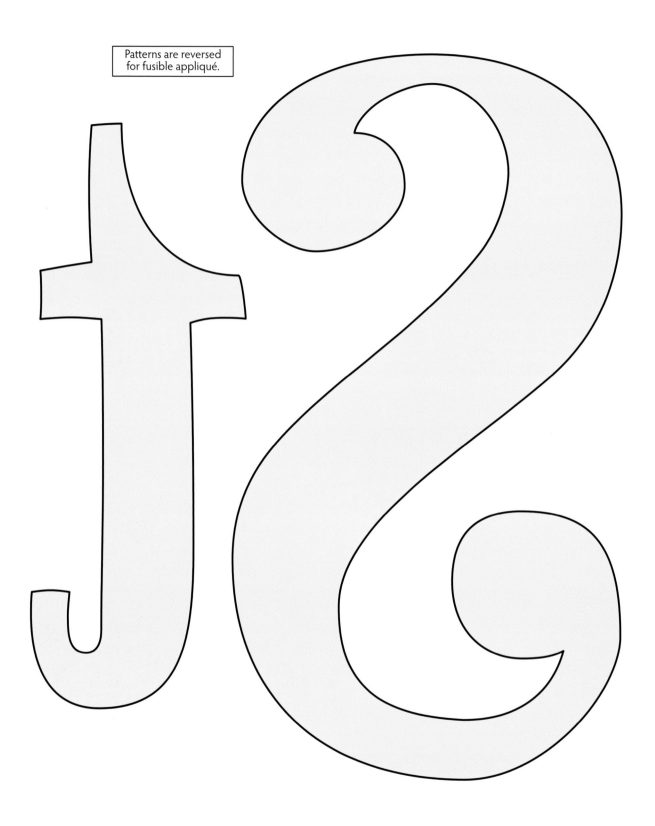

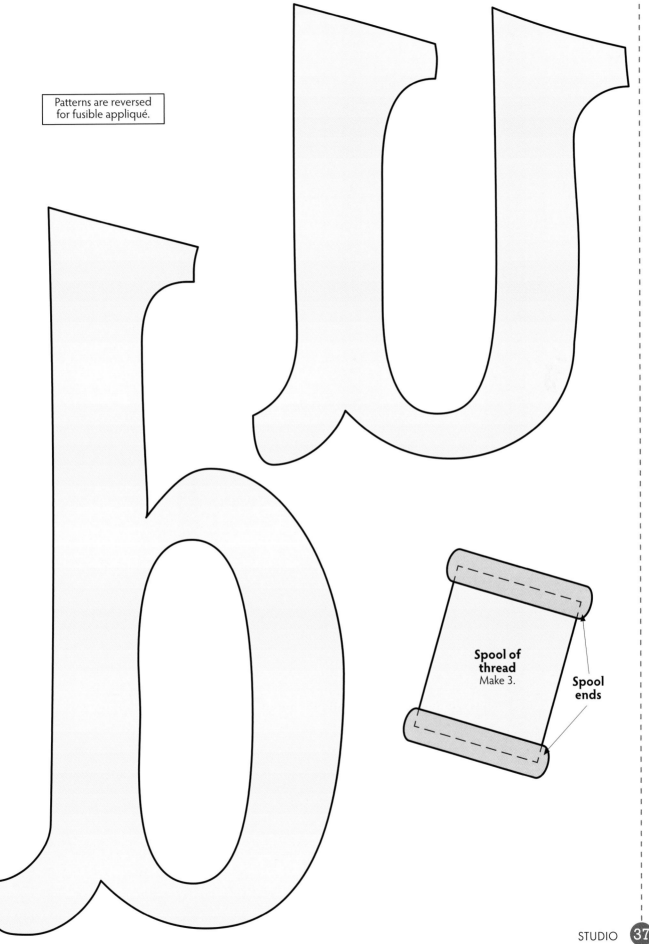

Patterns are reversed
for fusible appliqué.

**Spool of
thread**
Make 3.

**Spool
ends**

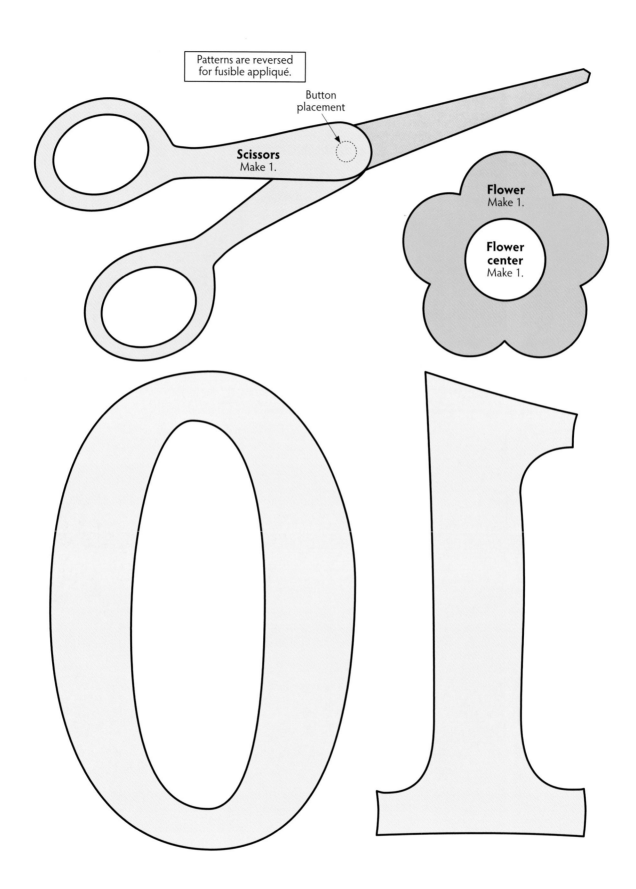

Patterns are reversed for fusible appliqué.

Button placement

Scissors
Make 1.

Flower
Make 1.

Flower center
Make 1.

Thank You, Teacher

Pick your most delicious red and green scraps and make a thank-you apple that the teacher can enjoy the whole school year.

Finished Quilt: 10" x 12"

PLAYGROUND METHODS USED

* Building Bits and Bobs (page 9) for apple and leaves
* Freezer-Paper Templates (page 14) for apple and leaves
* Bias-Covered Edges (page 17) for apple and leaves

Materials

1 fat quarter of white print for background
⅜ yard of red fabric for photo-album corners and binding
⅛ yard of green fabric for borders
Scraps of assorted red fabrics for patchwork apple*
Scraps of assorted green fabrics for patchwork leaves
1 fat quarter of fabric for backing
14" x 16" piece of batting
½ yard of ⅜"-wide ribbon for hanging
2 red buttons, 1" diameter, for hanging
1 red button, ⅝" diameter, for apple
Small scrap of brown Ultrasuede or felt for stem
¼"-wide paper-backed fusible tape
Freezer paper
¼" bias-tape maker
Fabric glue

You may want to include a yellow fabric, like I did.

Cutting

From the white print, cut:
1 rectangle, 8" x 10"

From the ⅛ yard of green fabric, cut:
2 strips, 1¾" x 9½"
2 strips, 1¾" x 10"
15" of ⅝"-wide bias strips

From the ¼ yard of red fabric, cut:
4 squares, 3" x 3"
18" of ⅝"-wide bias strips
50" of 2"-wide bias strips

Making the Appliqué Elements

1. Use the Freezer-Paper Templates method and the patterns on page 43 to make templates for the apple and each leaf. (Even if you've used freezer-paper templates before, please refer to the information on page 14 for how they are used in this project.)

2. Using the Building Bits and Bobs method, make a red fabric composition for the apple and a green fabric composition large enough for both leaves.

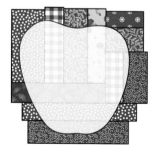 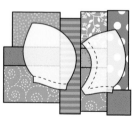

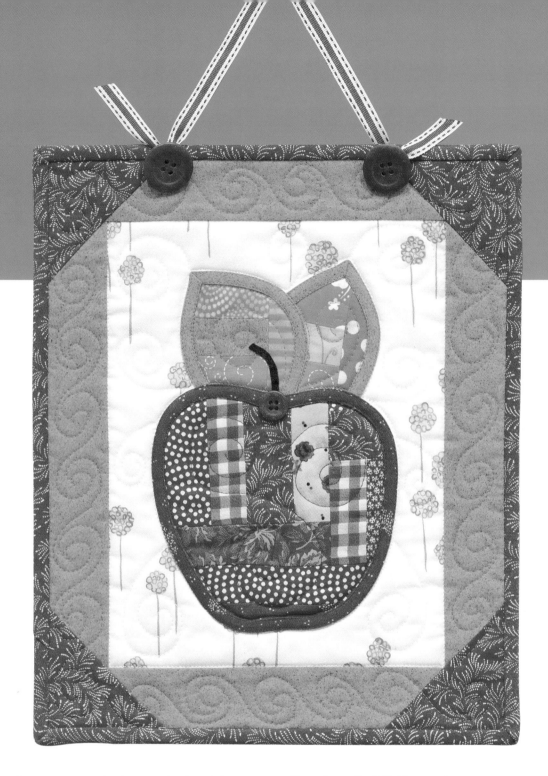

3. Use the Bias-Covered Edges method and the ⅝"-wide red and green bias strips to make fusible bias tape for covering the edges of the apple and leaves.

4. Iron the freezer-paper templates to the right side of the appropriate patchwork composition.

5. Cut out the elements exactly on the solid lines. When cutting out the leaves, be sure to leave extra fabric beyond the dashed lines.

Putting It All Together

1. Remove the freezer-paper templates and place the appliqué elements on the background fabric. Remove the apple for now. Apply a few tiny dots of fabric glue under the raw edges of the leaves to hold them in place.

2. Fuse the green bias tape to the leaves, covering their raw edges and molding the tape along the

curves. At the tip of each leaf, fold the tape into a miter.

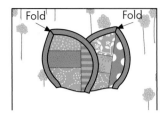

3. In the same manner, glue baste the apple in place and fuse the red bias tape on top of the raw edges, beginning and ending at the top of the apple. The raw ends of the bias tape will be covered by a button.

4. Edgestitch the motifs in place. I used matching thread and stitched down both sides of the bias tape.

5. Press and trim the quilt top to measure 7½" x 9½", keeping the design centered.

6. Sew the 9½"-long green strips to the sides of the quilt and press the seam allowances toward the border. Sew the 10"-long strips to the top and bottom of the quilt. Press the seam allowances toward the border.

7. To add the photo-album corners, use a pencil and ruler to draw a diagonal line on the wrong side of each 3" red square.

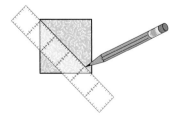

8. Place a marked square on each corner of the quilt as shown, right sides together and raw edges aligned. Stitch on the marked line.

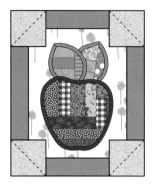

9. Flip the resulting triangles open; verify that the corners are stitched correctly and that the raw edges are aligned. Press. If desired, trim the excess corner fabric, leaving a ¼" seam allowance.

The Finish Line

1. Refer to "The Finish Line" on page 20 for information on how I finish my quilts. Layer, baste, and quilt the project. Add binding and a label.

2. Freehand cut a curved sliver of Ultrasuede or felt for the stem. Hand stitch in place. Sew the small button in place, covering the ends of the stem and bias tape.

3. Sew the two larger buttons along the top edge as shown in the photo on page 41. Add the ribbon for hanging.

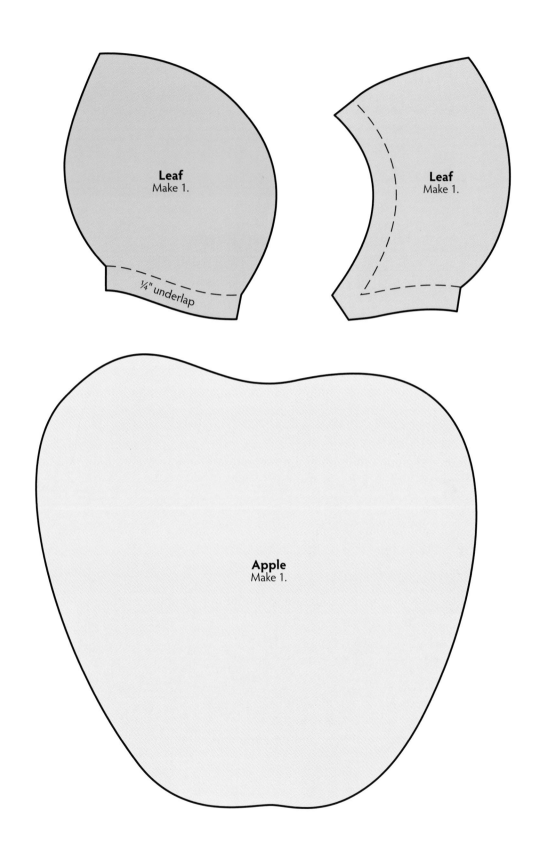

Leaf
Make 1.

¼" underlap

Leaf
Make 1.

Apple
Make 1.

Crazy Hearts

Don't plan too much when sewing the heart compositions together. Much of the fun comes from the delightful surprises you'll get!

Finished Quilt: 21½" x 21½" • Finished Block: 5½" x 5½"

PLAYGROUND METHODS USED

★ Crazy Patch (page 10) for hearts
★ Fusible-Web Templates (page 16) for hearts

Materials

Fat eighths measure 9" x 21".

½ yard of white-on-white fabric for background and inner border

4 fat eighths of assorted turquoise fabrics for blocks and outer border

Scraps of assorted turquoise fabrics, at least 2" x 2", for blocks

Scraps of assorted red and orange fabrics for patchwork hearts

Scrap of red fabric, at least 5" x 5", for outer-border corners

⅜ yard of fabric for binding

⅞ yard of fabric for backing

25" x 25" piece of batting

½ yard of 17"-wide lightweight paper-backed fusible web

Plain paper

Cutting

From the white-on-white fabric, cut:
9 squares, 6½" x 6½"
2 strips, 1¼" x 17"
2 strips, 1¼" x 18½"

From *each* of the turquoise fat eighths, cut:
2 strips, 2" x 9½" (8 total)

From the remaining turquoise fat eighths and the assorted turquoise scraps, cut a *total* of:
36 squares, 1½" x 1½"

From the 5" red scrap, cut:
4 squares, 2" x 2"

From the binding fabric, cut:
95" of 2"-wide bias strips

Making the Quilt Center

You'll build the Crazy-patch compositions, and then turn them into appliqué heart blocks. By adding scrappy triangles to the corners of the blocks, a mosaic diamond effect is created when the blocks are sewn together.

1. Trace the heart pattern on page 47 onto a piece of plain paper. Cut out the heart to make a paper template to use for sizing.

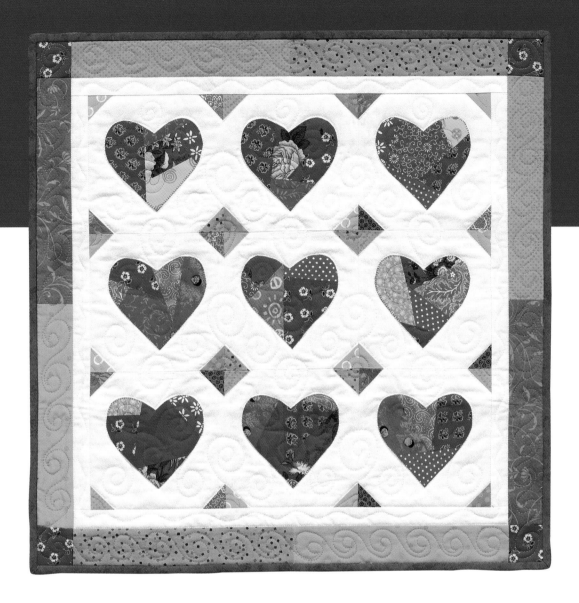

2. Use the Crazy Patch method and the assorted red and orange scraps to make nine patchwork compositions. Use the paper template to make sure the compositions are large enough for the heart shape.

Make 9.

3. Using the Fusible-Web Templates method, make nine heart appliqués. Center the hearts on the white background squares and fuse in place.

4. Blanket-stitch around each appliqué. Press the blocks and trim them to measure 6" x 6", keeping the hearts centered.

5. Using a pencil and ruler, draw a diagonal line on the wrong side of each 1½" turquoise square.

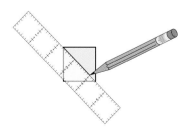

6. Place a marked square on each corner of a heart block as shown, right sides together and raw edges aligned. Stitch on the marked line.

7. Flip the resulting triangles open; verify that the corners are stitched correctly and that the raw edges are aligned. Trim the excess corner fabric, leaving a ¼" seam allowance. Flip the triangles back into place and press the seam allowances open.

8. Repeat steps 6 and 7 to make a total of nine blocks.

Putting It All Together

1. Lay out the blocks in three rows of three blocks each. When you are pleased with the arrangement, sew the blocks together into rows. Press the seam allowances open. Then sew the rows together and press the seam allowances open.

2. Sew the 17"-long white strips to opposite sides of the quilt top for the inner border. Press the seam allowances toward the border. Sew the 18½"-long white strips to the top and bottom of the quilt top. Press the seam allowances toward the border.

3. Join the turquoise strips end-to-end in pairs to make four outer-border strips. Press the seam allowances open. Sew two of the outer-border strips to opposite sides of the quilt top. Press the seam allowances toward the outer border.

4. Sew 2" red squares to both ends of the remaining two outer-border strips. Press the seam allowances toward the turquoise. Sew these borders to the top and bottom of the quilt top and press the seam allowances toward the outer border.

The Finish Line

Refer to "The Finish Line" on page 20 for information on how I finish my quilts. Layer, baste, and quilt the project. Add binding and a label.

Heart
Make 9.

Pop Beads

Groovy! Modern fabrics make bright and stylish Crazy-patch compositions. String these beads together for a look that's both retro and today!

Finished Quilt: 12½" x 20½"

PLAYGROUND METHODS USED
★ Crazy Patch (page 10) for bead circles
★ Fusible Interfacing (page 14) for bead circles

Materials

Fat quarters measure 18" x 21".

1 fat quarter of white print for background

1 fat quarter of blue fabric for connecting strings and binding

Scraps of assorted multicolored fabrics for patchwork circles

1 fat quarter of fabric for backing

16" x 24" piece of batting

⅜ yard of 20"-wide sheer to lightweight fusible interfacing

Thin cardboard

Chalk marker

Cutting

From the white print, cut:
6 strips, 2¼" x 21"

From the blue fabric, cut:
3 strips, 1" x 21"
75" of 2"-wide bias binding

Making the Background

Sew one blue strip between two light strips. Press the seam allowances toward the blue strip. Straighten one end and trim the unit to measure 20½" long. Repeat to make a total of three strip units.

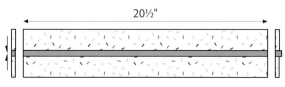

Make 3.

Making the Appliqué Elements

1. Use the pattern on page 50 and thin cardboard to make a circle template.

2. Use the Crazy Patch method and the multicolored scraps to make 17 patchwork compositions for the bead circles. Use the template to make sure each composition is larger than the circle.

3. Using the Fusible Interfacing method, the template, and the patchwork compositions, make 17 bead circles.

4. Choose four circles. Fold these circles in half and mark the centerline with a chalk line. Add ¼"

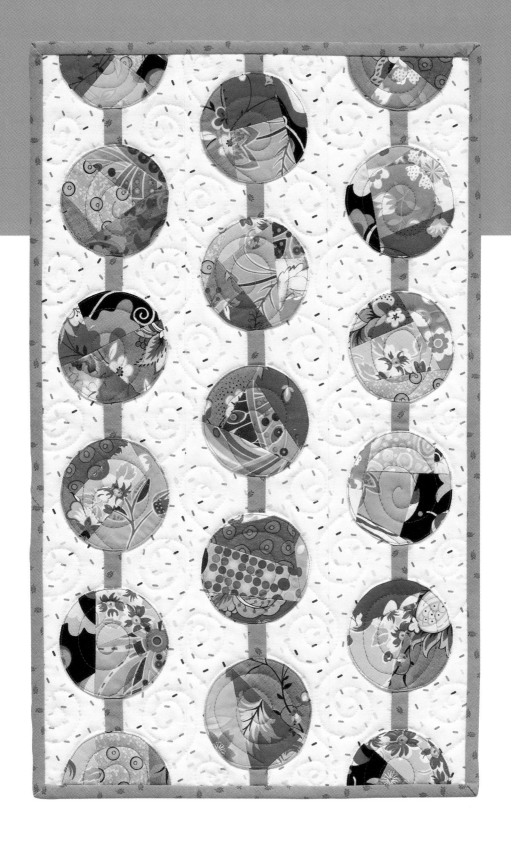

above the chalk line and cut off the rest of the circle. Make four partial circles.

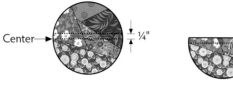

Center→ ¼"

Make 4.

Putting It All Together

1. On one of the strip units, position a partial circle on each end of the unit, with the straight edges aligned and the half circles centered on the blue strip. Position four circles 1" apart between the half circles, centering the circles on the blue strip. Fuse the circles in place. In the same manner, position and fuse two half circles and four circles onto a second strip unit.

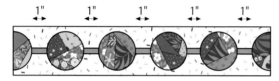

1" 1" 1" 1" 1"

Make 2.

2. On the remaining strip unit, position circles ¾" from each end of the unit and centered on the blue strip. Then position the remaining circles 1" apart, centering them on the blue strip. Fuse the circles in place.

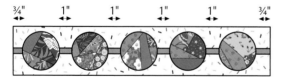

¾" 1" 1" 1" 1" ¾"

Make 1.

3. Edgestitch around each circle. To reduce bulk, trim away the background fabric from underneath each circle, leaving a ¼" seam allowance.

4. Sew the strip units together as shown in the photo on page 49. Press the seam allowances open.

The Finish Line

Refer to "The Finish Line" on page 20 for information on how I finish my quilts. Layer, baste, and quilt the project. Add binding and a label.

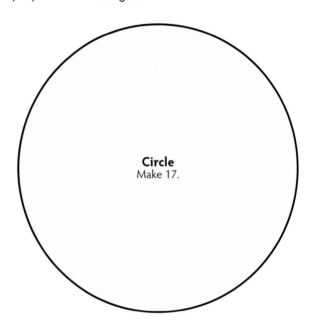

Circle
Make 17.

Flower Patch

Playground appliqué can be used for many motifs, including lovely flowers. Take any design to the playground!

Finished Quilt: 23¼" x 23¼" • Finished Blocks: 9" x 9"

PLAYGROUND METHODS USED

* Lay Down and Fuse (page 12) for patchwork appliqués
* Freezer-Paper Templates (page 14) for patchwork appliqués
* Fusible-Web Templates (page 16) for plain appliqués

Materials

Fat eighths measure 9" x 21".

⅜ yard of white-on-white fabric for background

1 fat eighth of green fabric for sashing

Assorted scraps of blue fabrics, at least 3" x 8", for border

Scrap of pink fabric, at least 6" x 6", for photo-album corners

Scraps and strips of assorted pink, green, yellow, blue, and brown fabrics for patchwork appliqués, plain appliqués, and sashing square

⅜ yard **OR** scraps of assorted blue fabrics for binding

⅞ yard of fabric for backing

27" x 27" piece of batting

½ yard of 17"-wide lightweight paper-backed fusible web

Nonstick appliqué pressing sheet

Tracing paper

Freezer paper

Black marking pen

Cutting

From the white-on-white fabric, cut:
4 squares, 10" x 10"

From the fat eighth of green fabric, cut:
4 strips, 1¼" x 9½"

From the 6" pink scrap, cut:
4 squares, 2½" x 2½"

From the binding fabric, cut:
105" of 2"-wide bias binding

Making the Appliqué Elements

1. Using the patterns on pages 56–59 and a black marker, trace each appliqué pattern onto tracing paper to make a master pattern of each block; be sure to include the centering lines. Decide which shapes will be patched and which ones will not. I used plain fabrics to make the stems, coneflower heads, pot rims, cup handles, and flower centers. On the pattern, mark which shapes will be patchwork and which ones will be made from plain fabric.

2. For all of the patchwork shapes, use the Freezer-Paper Templates method to make freezer-paper templates. (Even if you've used this technique in the past, please refer to the information on page 14 for how it's used in this project.) A reversed pattern is not needed.

3. Trace all shapes that will come from the same fabric composition onto one piece of freezer paper, leaving at least ¼" between each shape. Use a dashed line to indicate any portion of a shape that will be overlapped by another shape. Number the shapes as indicated on the patterns.

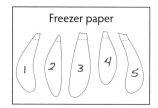

4. Use the Lay Down and Fuse method and a pressing sheet to make fabric compositions for the patchwork-appliqué motifs. Use the freezer-paper shape to verify that the composition is large enough.

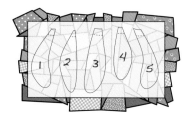

5. Let the composition cool and then carefully peel it from the pressing sheet. Lay the composition back down on the pressing sheet.

6. Position the appropriate freezer-paper template on top of the composition and press again to adhere the template to the fabric composition.

7. Peel the fabric composition and freezer-paper template together from the pressing sheet.

8. Cut out each shape exactly on the drawn solid lines, leaving at least ¼" beyond the dashed lines. Leave the template on the fabric shape

until you're ready to position the appliqué elements on the background fabric.

9. Using the Fusible-Web Templates method, prepare the plain-fabric appliqué motifs. Remember that the fusible-web method requires a reversed pattern, so flip the master patterns over and trace these templates from the reverse side.

Assembling the Blocks

1. Fold the white squares horizontally and vertically into quarters and crease the outer edges to create centering marks.

2. For each block, place the master pattern, right side up, underneath the white square. Line up the creases in the fabric with the centering lines on the pattern.

3. Using the master pattern as a placement guide, remove the freezer-paper templates and the fusible-web paper backing; then place the motifs on the white background, starting with the leaves and stems. For the coneflowers, the placement of the petals doesn't need to be exact. It doesn't matter which petals overlap or are spread apart from one another.

4. When satisfied with the placement, remove the master pattern. Following the manufacturer's recommendations, steam press the appliqué pieces until they're fused to the background. Don't move the iron back and forth across the motifs; just pick up the iron and put it down until all sections are fused.

5. Blanket-stitch around the edges of the motifs. I used thread that blended with the general color of each motif. Trim the blocks to measure 9½" x 9½", keeping the designs centered.

Putting It All Together

1. Sew a green strip between two appliquéd blocks, making sure the blocks are oriented in the same direction. Press the seam allowances toward the green strip. Make two of these rows, referring to the photo on page 53 as needed for placement guidance.

2. From the remaining pink scraps, cut one 1¼" square. Sew the pink square between two remaining green strips. Press the seam allowances toward the green strips.

3. Matching the seam intersections, sew the block rows from step 1 and sashing row from step 2 together. Press the seam allowances toward the sashing row.

4. Cut the assorted blue strips into varying lengths, from about 5" to 8" long. Lay out the pieces as desired to frame the quilt. Sew the pieces together, and then trim the two side borders to measure 2½" x 19¼" long. Trim the top and bottom borders to measure 2½" x 23¼" long.

5. Sew the borders to the sides, top, and bottom of the quilt. Press the seam allowances toward the just-added border.

6. Using a pencil and ruler, draw a diagonal line on the wrong side of each 2½" pink square. Place a marked square on each corner of the blue outer border, right sides together and raw edges aligned as shown below. Stitch on the marked line.

7. Flip the resulting triangles open; verify that the corners are stitched correctly and that the raw edges are aligned. Trim the excess corner fabric, leaving a ¼" seam allowance. Flip the triangles back into place and press the seam allowances toward the pink triangle.

The Finish Line

Refer to "The Finish Line" on page 20 for information on how I finish my quilts. Layer, baste, and quilt the project. Add binding and a label.

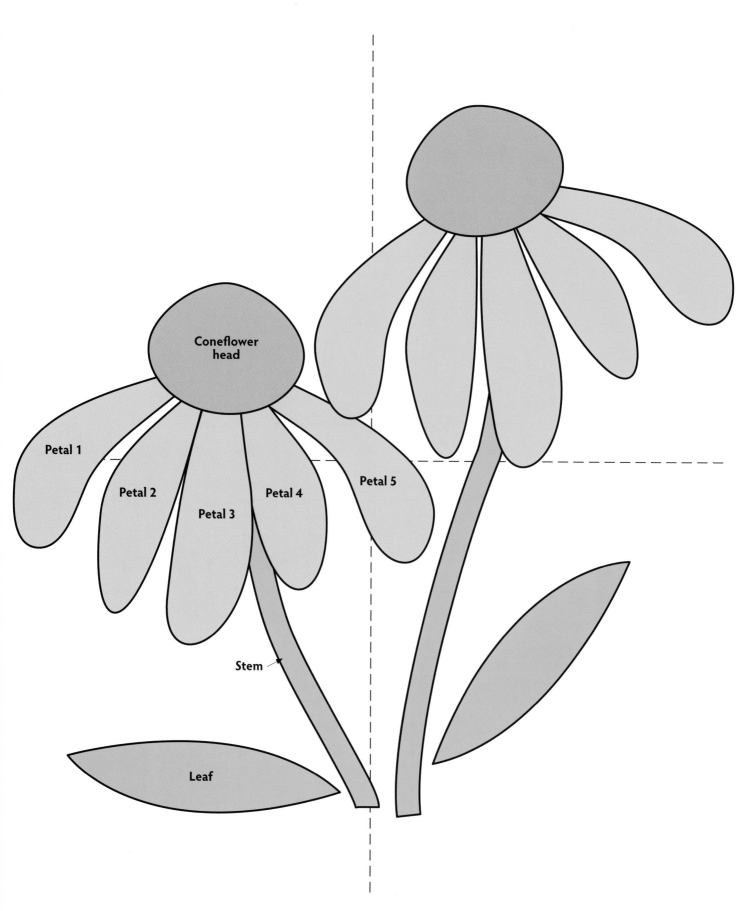

Coneflower head

Petal 1

Petal 2

Petal 3

Petal 4

Petal 5

Stem

Leaf

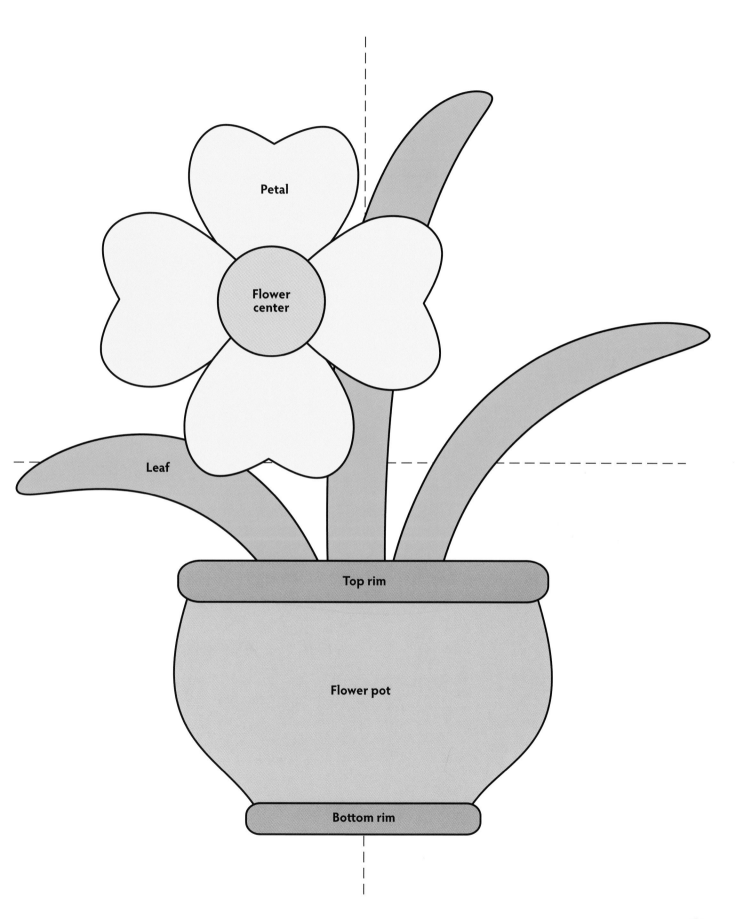

Petal

Flower
center

Leaf

Top rim

Flower pot

Bottom rim

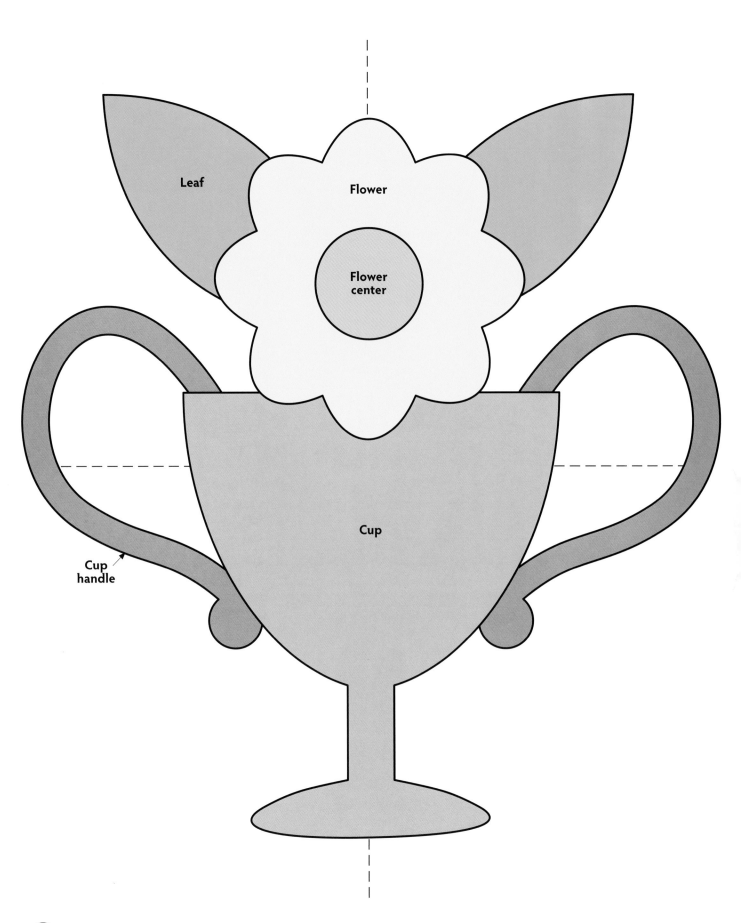

Leaf

Flower

Flower center

Cup

Cup handle

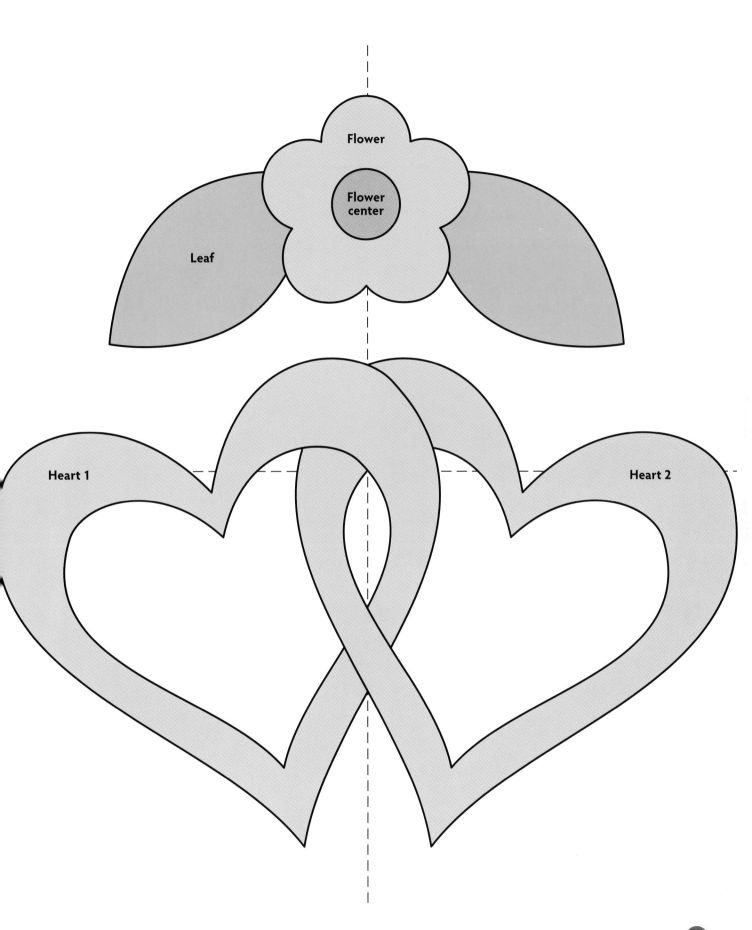

Flower

Flower
center

Leaf

Heart 1

Heart 2

Imaginary Blooms

Let your imagination grow. Patch together some beautiful batiks and freehand cut your flowers! If you'd like to make the ones that I cooked up, I've provided the full-size patterns.

Finished Quilt: 16" x 12"

PLAYGROUND METHODS USED

* Lay Down and Fuse (page 12) for flowers and leaves

* Freezer-Paper Templates (page 14) for flowers and leaves

* Fusible-Web Templates (page 16) for circles, stems, and other small elements as desired

Materials

Fat quarters measure 18" x 21".

1 fat quarter of black fabric for background
Scraps of assorted orange, blue, pink, green, red, and yellow for patchwork appliqués
³⁄₈ yard of fabric for binding
1 fat quarter of fabric for backing
16" x 20" piece of batting
¼ yard of 17"-wide lightweight paper-backed fusible web
Freezer paper
Nonstick appliqué pressing sheet
Chalk marker

Cutting

From the black fabric, cut:
1 rectangle, 17" x 13"

From the binding fabric, cut:
70" of 2"-wide bias binding

Making the Appliqué Elements

1. Using the Fusible-Web Templates method and the patterns on pages 62 and 63, prepare the plain-fabric appliqué motifs. I used this method for the spiky points on the sunburst flower, the yellow parts of the tulip bloom, the circles on all three flowers, and the three stems. Patterns for the asymmetrical stems have been reversed for your convenience. Use a dashed line to indicate any portion of a shape that will be overlapped by another shape.

2. Using the Freezer-Paper Templates method and the patterns on page 63, make freezer-paper templates for the patchwork flowers and six leaves. On the spiral flower template, it's helpful to scribble inside the shape to make it easier to tell which part will be used for the flower and which part will be cut away. (Even if you've used this technique in the past, please refer to the information on page 14 for how it's used in this project.) A reversed pattern is not needed for any of these motifs.

   Trace all shapes that will come from the same fabric composition, such as the leaves,

onto one piece of freezer paper. Leave at least ¼" between each shape.

3. Use the "Lay Down and Fuse" method to create fabric compositions for the flowers and leaves. Use the freezer-paper templates to make sure each composition is larger than the template.

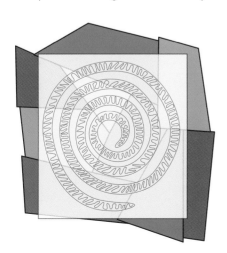

4. Let the compositions cool and then gently peel them from the pressing sheet. Lay the fabric compositions back down on the pressing sheet, one at a time.

5. Position the appropriate freezer-paper template on top of the composition and press again to adhere the template to the composition. Allow the piece to cool.

6. Peel the fabric composition and freezer-paper template together from the pressing sheet.

7. Repeat steps 5 and 6 for each fabric composition.

8. Cut out each shape exactly on the drawn solid lines. Leave the template on the fabric shape until you're ready to position the appliqué elements on the background fabric.

Putting It All Together

1. Use the chalk marker to mark the finished dimensions of the quilt, 16" x 12", on the black rectangle.

2. Remove the freezer-paper templates and the fusible-web paper backing. Position the elements on the background, keeping the elements at least ½" inside the finished-size markings. The spiral flower will be very floppy! Handle it gently and tease it into place.

3. Following the manufacturer's recommendations, fuse all of the elements in place.

4. Blanket-stitch around each element. I used thread that blended with the general color of each motif.

5. Press and trim the project.

The Finish Line

Refer to "The Finish Line" on page 20 for information on how I finish my quilts. Layer, baste, and quilt the project. Add binding and a label.

Reversed

Sunburst stem

Sunburst

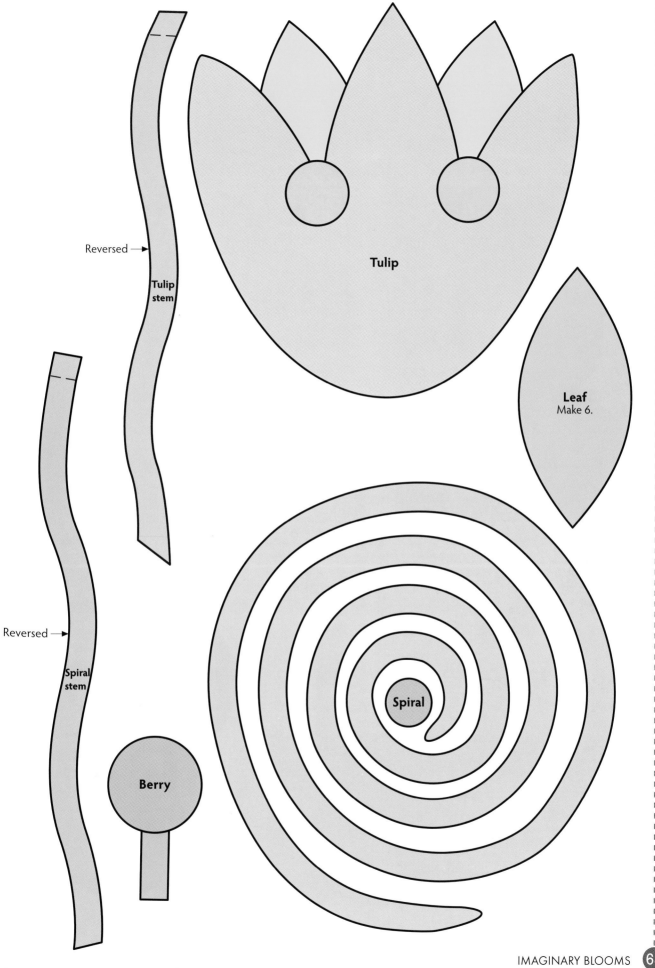

Reversed

Tulip stem

Reversed

Spiral stem

Tulip

Leaf
Make 6.

Spiral

Berry

About the Author

gregory case photography

While living in central Ohio as a newlywed, Kay took one class and became an instant quilter. She was an appliqué enthusiast from the get-go!

A few years later, fortune took the Mackenzies to Santa Cruz, California, where Kay now lives with her husband of more than two decades, science journalist Dana Mackenzie.

Classes in digital media at the local college introduced Kay to computer illustration, and again it was love at first try. Appliqué design and computer drawing—what a great combo platter! Combine them with a writerly bent and, according to Kay, you've got the best job in the world!

Kay is the author of *Inspired by Tradition: 50 Appliqué Blocks in 5 Sizes* (Martingale & Company, 2011).

Kay blogs about appliqué at www.allaboutapplique.net. Visit her there and also at her website, www.kaymackenzie.com.